I0141430

ONE. LESS. STONE.

Books by Tim Barker

Anticipating the Return of Christ

At Your Feet

Called Camp 2025

Discovering God in the Secret Places

End Times

God's Revelation and Your Future

It's Not All About Sitting at the Head Table

Mighty Men of Courage from the Bible

My Jesus Journey

My Jesus Journey: Crescendo

My Jesus Journey: Glissando

My Jesus Journey: Rhapsody

Names of God

Open Doors

Our Privilege of Joy

Reflecting Christ Through the Fruit of the Spirit

The Authentic Christian: Revealing Christ through the Fruit of the Spirit

The Call of Ephesians

The Lord with Us

The Twelve: Taking Up the Mantle of Christ

The Vision of Nehemiah: God's Plan for Righteous Living

Truth, Love & Redemption: The Holy Spirit for Today

Unified Church

Your Invitation to Christ

ONE. LESS. STONE.

Tim R. Barker, D. Min.

Network Pastor/Superintendent
South Texas Ministry Network

ONE. LESS. STONE., Barker, Tim.

1st ed.

Unless otherwise noted, Scriptures are taken from the New International Version (NIV): Scripture taken from The Holy Bible, New International Version ®. Copyright© 1973, 1978, 1984, 2011 by Biblica, Inc.™. Used by permission of Zondervan.

Scriptures marked NKJV are taken from the NEW KING JAMES VERSION (NKJV): Scripture taken from the NEW KING JAMES VERSION®. Copyright© 1982 by Thomas Nelson, Inc. Used by permission. All rights reserved.

This book and its contents are wholly the creation and intellectual property of Tim Barker.

This book may not be reproduced in whole or in part, by electronic process or any other means, without written permission of the author.

ISBN: 979-8-9924875-4-1

Copyright © 2025 by Tim Barker

All Rights Reserved

Dedication

I was raised in a church where worship was vibrant and expressive—I didn't realize that wasn't the norm for every congregation until I experienced more reserved styles. I deeply love Jesus and cherish the freedom to worship Him without restraint.

This book is lovingly dedicated to my precious spiritual children, Pastors John and Chidinma Aniemeke, and to my Bethel Covenant Assembly of God family in San Antonio. You continually remind me of what genuine, passionate worship looks like.

Though I may not match your energy in dance or outward expression, my heart is fully engaged. You inspire me, and I am confident that your worship brings joy to our Father. May we never lose the wonder and boldness of worshipping God for who He is.

Tim R. Barker

Contents

Introduction

The praise service on Sunday morning …

We act like it's a buffer to the real service, an intermission where pretty music is playing, but if we need to get something done, then that's the time for us to prepare for the real service.

We even factor in the praise and worship time if we're running late to church. Yes, we have time to stop for breakfast … gas up the car … run back to the house for the umbrella we forgot to grab. After all, it's only the worship team. It's not like it's the real ministry opportunity.

God's Word begs to differ.

Our heartfelt praise is a weapon against worry and the attacks of the evil one. The praise and worship team leads us by breaking down the walls and casting off the chains of our weekly worries. Our active praise motivates us into obedience and empowers us to step out in strength with the joy of Jesus on our lips.

We owe God our praise, even if we don't feel it inside. When we shake the walls with our praise, and we worship God wholeheartedly, the atmosphere shifts, and our church service takes on new meaning.

Our praise then assumes a guiding role and serves as a prophecy for our future. It places the promise we cannot see into our grasp and gives us personal motivation and encouragement to walk in sanctification.

When we develop a personal lifestyle of passionate, daily praise, the stones will no longer be required to cry out to heaven, because we will have fulfilled Christ's command.

— I —

The Silent Threat
of the Stones

People Praising, Pharisees Grumbling

Then, as He was now drawing near the descent of the Mount of Olives, the whole multitude of the disciples began to rejoice and praise God with a loud voice for all the mighty works they had seen … And some of the Pharisees called to Him from the crowd, "Teacher, rebuke Your disciples." But He answered and said to them, *"I tell you that if these should keep silent, the stones would immediately cry out."*

— Luke 19:37-40 NKJV —

Imagine this moment:

Jerusalem is swelling with anticipation. Dust swirls around sandals. Voices shout. Branches wave.

It's not just a crowd. It's a revolution of worship.

Jesus Entering Jerusalem

And here comes Jesus, riding not a war horse but a humble donkey, surrounded not by soldiers but by shouting saints. People have seen too much to stay silent.

They can't help but cry out:

"Blessed is the King who comes in the name of the Lord!"

But then, cue the killjoys. The Pharisees step in with their polished robes and pious postures. They say:

"Jesus, tell your followers to tone it down!"

And Jesus responds with thunder:

"If they stay silent, the stones will cry out."

Stop Right There

Jesus just made a declaration that shakes the very soil:

"If they don't praise Me, creation will."

The praise must happen, with or without you. The question is:

Will you give it, or will a rock take your place?

Praise Has a Deadline

There's an expiration date on your silence. The moment you withhold what God is due, nature will step in.

Creation is watching you. The stones are listening. Heaven is leaning in.

If you get too dignified, too distracted, or too discouraged to praise ... God will get glory anyway.

I don't want a backup singer made of granite singing my song.

I don't want a rock altar to wear the praise I was created to release. That's one less stone, and it won't be mine.

Stones Are Standing By

Here's the threat:

The rocks are on standby.

Creation is pre-programmed to respond to its Creator.

Psalm 96 says the trees will clap their hands.

Isaiah says mountains and hills will burst into song. Even seas will roar, and the fields will rejoice.

And if mankind, which has experienced redemption, resurrection, and restoration, goes mute, then the rocks will do what we won't.

But let me be clear:

I've been forgiven too much to go quiet. I've survived too much to whisper. I've walked through fire and didn't burn, so that stone can sit back down.

The Call to the Church

This isn't about personality.

It's about priority.

You don't have to be loud to be obedient, but you must be unashamed.

Jesus didn't say the Pharisees were wrong about the volume.

He said they were wrong about the value of praise.

Because praise isn't just expression. It's evidence.

It proves you're:

- Still alive.

- Still grateful.

- Still dangerous to the enemy's camp.

And if the enemy can't steal your salvation, he'll try to steal your sound.

But not today.

As Long as I Have Breath, I Will Not Surrender My Praise to a Rock!

Let every religious muzzle break.

Let every dignified silence shatter.

Let every dry stone be bypassed … because this

worshiper is wide awake.

You've got too much breath to stay quiet ... too much history to be casual.

Too much destiny to stay dry.

Don't let a rock take your place. That's ...

ONE. LESS. STONE.

"The devil isn't concerned about your church attendance. He's concerned about the volume of your praise."

Pray With Me

Jesus, thank You for allowing my soul to leap with joy for You.

I will dismiss the killjoys who would steal my praise for You, for only in You can I find true peace in my life.

Let me be observant to the world around me, for even in Nature, the lessons of Your beauty and bounty surround me.

I will not be a backup singer in my worship of You, nor will I turn down the volume of my praise.

In You I will rejoice forever. Amen.

Worship in Action

1. Jesus triggered praise from the people. Name something that triggers praise in you. Share it with someone.

2. A grateful nature is important in all areas of our lives. Share with someone a time you've been grateful for them.

3. Make a plan to start a new praise program in your church body. Invite others to join in.

— 2 —

When Rocks Start Stretching

On Standby to Praise

For we know that the whole creation groans and labors with birth pangs together until now.

— Romans 8:22 —

Let's get real:

Creation is not quiet. It's groaning, waiting, and stretching ...

... yearning for something it can't quite reach.

The Groaning of Creation

Romans 8 tells us that creation is groaning like a woman in labor.

Not because it's in rebellion, but because it's in anticipation.

It's not groaning in resistance ... it's groaning in expectation.

But why is creation groaning?

Because it's waiting for us, the sons and daughters of God, to take our rightful place.

It's waiting for the church to roar with revelation, not tiptoe in tradition.

It's waiting for the Bride to cry out again, not just with programs, but with power.

And if we stay silent ... if we remain dormant ... if we hold our breath ... the stones will start to stretch.

The Readiness of Creation

Jesus wasn't being poetic in Luke 19. He was

being prophetic.

The earth remembers the sound of Eden.

It remembers walking with God in the cool of the day.

It remembers Adam's footsteps … righteous, redeemed, and unbroken.

And now, after the fall, creation waits … groans … and reaches …

… just for a glimpse of the sons and daughters who carry that same authority.

Creation is wired to respond to worship.

Trees clap. Mountains tremble. Oceans roar. Earthquakes split the ground when glory shows up.

So, when you stay silent, it's not just a personal choice … it's a cosmic consequence.

Praise Delayed Is Praise Denied

Let's be blunt: delayed praise is disobedience.

When you feel the prompting to worship, and you suppress it with fear, pride, or fatigue, something else is standing in line behind you, ready to take your place.

Every second you withhold your praise is a second a rock stretches its mouth to cry out.

But let me declare it loud and bold:

I will not give my song to a stone.

That's my shout. That's my dance. That's my sound.

Praise Isn't Optional - It's Original

You weren't created to worry. You weren't created to stress.

You were created to praise.

That's why worship feels right. That's why shouting feels natural. That's why silence feels like suffocation ... because your spirit was born for sound.

Let everything that has breath praise the Lord.

— Psalm 150:6 —

And when the breath of God fills your lungs, the first thing that should leave them is glory.

The Danger of a Silent Church in a Loud World

If we choose not to lift our voices in praise, then the rocks are going to get louder than the redeemed … and we can't let that happen.

Creation is already in motion.

- The trees are clapping.
- The seas are roaring.
- The earth is stretching.

But as for me?

I'm not handing off my hallelujah.

Let creation stand down …

… because this is one less stone that will have to cry out.

THAT. ONE. STONE. STAYS. SILENT.

"A quiet church is a
defeated church. But a
praising church is a terror
to hell."

Pray With Me

Jesus, let my ears be like Yours.

May the sounds of the earth's praise ring out around me and incite me to join in with a cry of rejoicing.

When trouble comes, remind me that I am wired to worship You.

When I hear the trees clap, see the mountains tremble, and watch in awe as the oceans tumble onto the shore, let my own voice rise in adulation to You as my King.

I will praise You in my car, when I am walking, and as I prepare my meals. I will hand off my hallelujah to no one.

I will continually praise You. Amen.

Worship in Action

1. Think of the programs in your church. Which ones truly express praise to God?

2. Step into Nature. What do you see that is an expression of praise to God?

3. What can you do RIGHT NOW to show the world that you are not handing off the hallelujah due to your Creator?

— 3 —

Every Hallelujah Has
a History

Praise Is Personal

Let the redeemed of the Lord say so, whom
He has redeemed from the hand of the enemy.

— Psalm 107:2 —

You don't just praise God because the worship
leader tells you to.

You don't shout hallelujah because it's written on

the screen.

You praise because you remember.

You don't praise based on feelings; you praise based on what you've seen God do.

- There's history in your hallelujah.

- There's weight in your worship.

- There's a testimony in your shout.

Real praise is never empty.

- It's evidence.

- It carries the echo of past deliverance.

- It holds the memory of miracles, the timeline of triumphs, and the fingerprints of God's faithfulness.

Praise That's Been Through Something

Some people think praise is about volume.

But loud doesn't always mean deep ... and soft doesn't mean shallow.

Praise isn't measured by decibels. It's measured by depth.

True praise comes from people who've been through the valley and found God to be good anyway.

- It comes from people who buried loved ones and still lifted hands.

- From people who've heard no and shouted yes to God anyway.

- From people who were broke, beaten, and betrayed but still believed.

Praise is personal … intrinsic to the core of who we are. If I don't know your story, I can't possibly judge your shout.

Praise expresses the life, the trials, and the victories that God has brought us through.

Stones Can't Testify

This is why Jesus said the stones would cry out … but they can't testify.

A stone can groan. A stone can tremble. But a stone has never been healed.

A stone has never been saved.

A stone has never had chains broken.

But you have.

- You've been set free.

- You've been pulled out.

- You've been raised up.

You've got a history with the Healer.

So, when you praise, it's not noise …

… it's a news report.

Breaking News:

- I'm still here.

- And He is still good.

What Your Praise Says

Every time you lift your voice, you're sending a message to three realms:

To Heaven:

I remember. The mysteries of Your work in my life will never be forgotten.

To Hell:

I'm still here. My foot stands on the foundation

of the cross, and in Him I am victorious.

To Yourself:

He is not finished. The Father still has a work for me to do, and I FIND MY STRENGTH IN HIM.

Your praise says:

- I've seen too much to stay quiet.

- I've come too far to turn back now.

- I've got too much invested to let a stone take my place.

Your hallelujah has history.

- Don't hide it.

- Don't silence it.

- Don't sanitize it.

Your hallelujah needs to be spoken. It needs to be heard by those nearby. Your hallelujah needs to be shouted from the rooftops.

- Let the redeemed of the Lord SAY SO.

- Let the broken-but-healed SAY SO.

- Let the ones with scars and songs SAY SO.

In your lifestyle, in your giving, and in your relations with those around you …

- Say it loud.

- Say it again.

- Say it until the rocks stay silent.

Because every time you shout, it's one less stone that has to.

This is the truth you can never escape:

IF HE'S DONE ANYTHING FOR YOU—ANYTHING AT ALL—YOU'VE GOT A REASON TO SHOUT.

Power Proclamation

"My testimony took too
long for me to sit through
worship like nothing
happened."

Pray With Me

Jesus, remind me daily of my history with You.

Let my spoken words of praise be a testimony to Your goodness.

Others don't know my story, but You do. Teach me to be brave in my praise no matter how it looks to others.

I will stand with heaven as my backdrop, hell as my footstool, and my voice ringing out in praise to You.

Thank You for my history with You. Amen.

Worship in Action

1. Create a written history of God's victories in your life. Review them weekly.

2. Write out a praise plan. Speak your praise aloud. Say it again.

3. Invite your church body to participate in a group praise activity, such as:

   A markerboard in the church lobby . . .

   A Sunday evening praise service . . .

   A group praise page on the church website . . .

— 4 —

I Owe God a Praise That Granite Can't Give

Stones don't know grace

This people I have formed for Myself; they shall declare My praise.

— Isaiah 43:21 —

There's a sound that only the redeemed can release.

A song that only the blood-bought can sing.

A praise that no stone, no pillar, and no piece of pavement can ever produce.

Why?

- Because stones weren't delivered.

- They weren't forgiven.

- They weren't redeemed.

But you were.

- Granite never had guilt.

- Marble never knew mercy.

- But you … you were dead in sin and brought back to life.

And that means you owe God something that no rock can ever replicate.

Jesus didn't die for rocks.

He died for you.

Praise Is a Debt of Gratitude

We don't praise God to earn favor—we praise because we've already received it.

We're not paying a bill. We're responding to a

blessing.

David said to us:

What shall I render to the Lord for all His benefits toward me?

— Isaiah 43:21 —

In other words:

"How can I repay the God who saved my life?"

There is only one answer to David's question:

With praise.

- Praise is the tithe of your breath.

- It's the offering of your voice.

- It's the fruit of your lips. (Heb. 13:15)

You don't praise because life is easy. You praise because grace is amazing.

You can make this cry before God and the world, and the darkness will tremble before the mighty power of God's redemptive nature:

"I don't shout because I feel like it—I shout because I'm free."

Granite Has No Gospel

Let's say it again:

Rocks don't know the gospel.

- They've never felt shame.

- They've never tasted tears.

- They've never sat in a service, bound by chains, and walked out free.

But you have.

- You were lost but now you are found.

- Blind but now you see.

- Empty but now you are filled.

So, what does that mean?

It means your praise is irreplaceable.

- That stone might be strong, but it's not saved.

- That stone might be solid, but it's not sanctified.

- That stone cannot take my place or yours when it is time to raise our voices in worship before the God of the heavens.

You Are the Praise That God Wants

God isn't looking for polished worship.

He's looking for personal worship.

- Not rocks.

- Not statues.

- Not echoes.

He's looking for the sound of a person who knows what they were … and knows who they are now.

You don't have to be perfect to praise—you just have to be redeemed.

- You are His people.

- You are His voice in the earth.

So, lift it.

When the rocks start rattling …

When the ground starts groaning …

When creation starts rising …

Let it be known:

WE GOT HERE FIRST.

- That praise? It's mine.

- That shout? It's mine.

- That glory? It's mine to give.

Granite can't have my hallelujah. Marble can't carry my melody.

The stones can sit this one out.

Because ... THE REDEEMED ARE RISING.

And that's one less stone that has to.

THE. REDEEMED. MUST. NEVER. GO. QUIET.

Power Proclamation

"I've been bought with
blood—how dare I give
Him silence?"

Pray With Me

Jesus, thank You for bestowing Your favor upon me.

Remind me daily that my praise isn't to curry Your favor but because I already have it.

I offer my praise as a tithe of the blessing You have bestowed on me.

When life is hard, I will praise You. When I don't feel like it, I will praise You.

I will be Your voice of rejoicing in the earth. Amen.

Worship in Action

1. Place a stone on your desk or windowsill. Attach a note that says: "I am quiet because (your name) is not."

2. Prepare a gratitude list. Place it in your Bible to remind yourself of your debt of gratitude to the Lord.

3. Tell someone of the good they've done in your life. Let your attitude of praise extend to every interaction with people around you.

— 5 —

The Sound That Breaks Chains

Praise as Spiritual Warfare

Chains don't respond to cute praise. Lighthearted verses with catchy tunes, viral signs over our kitchen sink, or upbeat bumper stickers won't do the trick.

Chains break in response to costly praise.

But at midnight Paul and Silas were praying and singing hymns to God, and the prisoners were listening to them. Suddenly there was a great earthquake, so that the foundations of the prison were shaken; and immediately all the doors were opened and everyone's chains were loosed.

— Acts 16:25-26 —

There's a sound hell fears, and it's not your preaching.

It's not your résumé.

It's not your education.

It's your praise.

How Your Worship Shifts the Atmosphere

When Paul and Silas were locked in a prison cell, beaten, bruised, and bloodied, they didn't wait for their freedom to worship.

- They didn't wait for the verdict to change.

- They didn't wait for the pain to pass.

They lifted up a song in the midnight hour—the darkest time. And that sound broke open something in the spirit realm.

"Suddenly there was a great earthquake …"

"Immediately all the doors were opened …"

"Everyone's chains were loosed …"

Praise did what keys couldn't. Praise did what force wouldn't. Praise did what religion didn't.

Praise Isn't a Performance—It's a Prison Break

This kind of praise doesn't start on the stage.

It starts in the spirit.

- It's not polished.

- It's not practiced.

It's powerful.

- It doesn't need instruments … it needs intention.

- It doesn't wait for a worship leader … it just needs a willing vessel.

This praise shakes foundations.

- It opens doors.

- It sets captives free.

Some of the loudest breakthroughs begin with the softest whispers of worship.

Chains Don't Respond to Silence

Let's be honest.

- Chains don't fall off when you sit still.

- They don't break when you fold your arms.

- They don't move when you spectate.

Chains ...

... respond to sound.

... respond to authority.

... respond to heaven's frequency.

Praise is heaven's language of liberty.

You don't praise because you're free—you praise until you are.

Don't Wait—Worship Now

Don't wait for your situation to change ... change the atmosphere with your sound.

Don't wait for the doctor's report ... sing before the diagnosis.

Don't wait for the money to come in … praise Him on the promise.

Midnight praise leads to morning freedom.

Because sometimes your shout isn't for you …

… it's for someone else's chains.

Paul and Silas weren't the only ones who were freed. Everyone's chains came off.

Your praise might be the key to someone else's breakthrough.

- Praise is the sound that breaks chains.

- Praise is the sound that opens doors.

- Praise is the sound that destroys darkness.

Praise is not just a sound from your lips but from your life.

When you lift up praise not only in your voice but in every facet of daily living, you exemplify a life that says:

"I trust You even here."

"I'll praise You even now."

"I'll worship You even in this cell."

And when you do, earthquakes of change will rattle your situation. Foundations will shake, and doors will fall open.

Chains will fall, and you will be set free.

And that, my friend, is one less stone that has to cry out, all because you found your song, and it set somebody free.

YOUR PRAISE WILL SET OTHERS FREE!

Power Proclamation

"If walls don't shake when you praise, maybe you're just singing."

Pray With Me

Jesus, I want my voice to be a sound that hell fears.

I want to sing in my trials and lift Your praises in my darkest hours.

I don't need the key to release my chains … my praise to You has already done that.

Direct my prayers and reorder my thoughts. Let me see Your answers before they manifest and praise You for them.

Let me live in the expectation that the foundations under my feet will shake and my chains will fall away when I praise You. Amen.

Worship in Action

1. Choose a praise song. Sing it with sincerity as a worship offering to God.

2. Make a list of the chains in your life. Cross them off as you see them fall away.

3. Share your praise victories with a trusted believer. Add a stone to your windowsill for each new broken chain.

— 6 —

Religion Wants Silence—
Revival Demands Sound

The Pharisees' Attempt to Quiet the People

*And some of the Pharisees called to Him
from the crowd, "Teacher, rebuke Your disciples." But He answered and said to them, "I
tell you that if these should keep silent, the
stones would immediately cry out."*

— Luke 19:39-40 —

Religious Spirits vs. Revelatory Praise

Religion has always tried to muzzle revival.

- It's uncomfortable with shouting.

- It's suspicious of weeping.

- It's irritated by passion.

The Pharisees didn't rebuke Jesus for teaching. They rebuked Him for allowing praise.

Because nothing terrifies a religious spirit more than a loud, unashamed, Spirit-filled worshiper who refuses to be silenced.

Religion says, "Shhhh . . ."

Revival says, "SHOUT!"

Religion Prefers Order Over Outpouring

Let's be real:

Religious spirits love control.

They prefer predictable programs over unpredictable presence. They'd rather see decency than deliverance.

But revival doesn't follow the church bulletin.

It doesn't ask permission from the structure of the morning service.

It breaks in when it hears hunger.

That's why blind Bartimaeus got his miracle … because he wouldn't be quiet.

When he was hushed by those around him, he cried out even louder!

Real revival doesn't whisper. It roars.

You Can't Sanitize the Spirit

- You can dress it up.

- You can trim the altar call.

- You can lower the volume.

But when the Holy Spirit shows up, somebody is going to shout.

- Pentecost was noisy.

- The Upper Room was thunderous.

- The early church wasn't silent.

The early church was supernatural. It was infused with praise, with worship, and with voices raised to

God!

You can't have a Book of Acts movement with a Pharisee mouth.

God Is Raising Up a Noisy Remnant

There's a new generation rising—not of fans, but firebrands. They're not here for dead religion.

They're here to set altars on fire.

They don't care if it's messy. They care if it's anointed.

They aren't waiting for permission. They're carrying praise as a weapon.

And they're not scared of volume ... they're scared of losing their voice.

This move of God will not be muted.

The Difference Between Noise and Anointed Sound

Religion may prefer silence—but heaven responds to sound. If you want a sanitized church, you'll get sanitized results. But if you want a supernatural church—you had better get loud.

So let the Pharisees grumble. Let the dignified stare.

Let the cold, religious establishment criticize my fervent praise. Let them look down upon me for being noisy.

As for me?

- I'm going to shout until the walls fall.

- I'm going to dance until my chains break.

- I'm going to sing until the stones at my feet stay silent.

Revival has a sound …

… and I refuse to let a religious spirit steal it.

That's one less stone …

… and one more voice that hell can't silence.

YOUR VOICE MATTERS TO GOD!

Power Proclamation

"If your shout doesn't offend the stiff-necked, you're probably doing it wrong."

Pray With Me

Jesus, let me refuse to muzzle revival in my life.

Let me cast off religious dogma and let my heart rejoice in You.

When the world tries to silence me, let me cry out with a Bartimaeus voice for You!

Let me invite revival into my praise life, my family life, and my relationship with You.

Let me silence the stones with my shout of praise to You! Amen.

Worship in Action

1. Take your praise voice to your phone. Record a missed call message INVITING OTHERS TO PRAISE HIM.

2. Ramp up your praise at mealtimes by asking family members to share a word of praise during your prayer.

3. Make sure that everyone in your household can hear you in your prayer closet as you PRAISE GOD WITH GUSTO.

— 7 —

Thermostat Christians

___

Are You a Thermometer or a Thermostat?

You are the light of the world. A city that is set on a hill cannot be hidden ... Let your light so shine before men, that they may see your good works and glorify your Father in heaven.

— Matthew 5:14-16 —

There are two types of people in every room:

thermometers and thermostats.

- Thermometers measure the atmosphere.

- Thermostats set the atmosphere.

Inside the church, we can state it like this:

- Thermometers reflect the room.

- Thermostats redirect the room.

In this hour, God isn't looking for silent, temperature-taking saints.

He's looking for fire-starters who walk into dry places and release glory.

Or, as God would say to you if He walked into the room:

"If the atmosphere doesn't shift when you show up—you're blending in, not breaking through."

Don't Just Reflect It—Reform It

The world is loud about everything except truth.

Culture is setting the tone with:

- chaos

- fear

- anxiety

- compromise

Too many believers are just echoing what's already there.

Here's the vital truth you need to get from this chapter:

God didn't call you to reflect hell's volume. He called you to release heaven's voice.

- You are the salt of the earth.

- The light of the world.

- A city on a hill.

So, stop whispering. You are called to shift the atmosphere, not reflect what is already there.

Praise That Changes the Temperature

When you praise, you're not just making noise …

… you're turning the dial.

- Praise heats up cold hearts.

- Praise burns away apathy.

- Praise melts spiritual icicles off dead churches.

Your worship can take a room:

- From routine to revival.

- From frozen to fire.

- From complacent to consumed.

Praise doesn't just fill space. It transforms it.

Carry Yourself with Authority

Kick your timid steps out the door. Cast off the weakness you've carried. You are commissioned by the God of all creation.

You are:

- Anointed.

- Authorized.

- Activated.

The same Spirit that raised Jesus from the dead lives in you. And when you show up, darkness should get nervous.

You're not a churchgoer. You're a thermostat.

So ... adjust the room.

- Raise the fire.

- Break the silence.

- Shift the atmosphere.

Toss out the old you.

- No more passive presence.

- No more silent saints.

- No more lukewarm gatherings.

God is raising a church that doesn't just survive the room—it sets the room. He wants a people that walks in burning with heaven's temperature and turns up the heat for everyone else.

- So, if you've got fire—release it.

- If you've got a shout—let it out.

- If you've got praise—don't postpone it.

This room is waiting to be shifted.

As long as I've got breath to change the climate ...

THAT'S ONE LESS STONE THAT HAS TO.

Power Proclamation

"I didn't come to reflect the room—I came to shift it."

Pray With Me

Jesus, I choose to be a thermostat for You.

I ask You to burn inside me and keep me on fire for You!

No matter the temperature in the room, let my praise be loud and raucous. When I lift my hands, let Your power spill out onto those around me.

Anoint, authorize, and activate my praise to embolden the church to step up for You!

I refuse to be passive. I refuse to be silent. I refuse to be lukewarm in Your presence! Amen.

Worship in Action

1. Write the name of someone you see as a thermostat in your church. Tell them what they mean to you.

2. Look for situations where you can be an example for others to follow. Then volunteer, step up, and be there for them.

3. How can you break your silence and avoid becoming a lukewarm believer? Challenge a fellow believer to stand with you in releasing the fire of praise.

— 8 —

Praise Is More Than Volume—It's a Weapon

What Happens in the Spirit World When You Praise

And when he had consulted with the people, he appointed those who should sing to the Lord ...

Now when they began to sing and to praise, the Lord set ambushes against the people … who had come against Judah; and they were defeated.

— 2 Chronicles 20:21–22 —

Too many people think praise is just the opening act of a church service.

It's not the warm-up. *It's the warfare.*

When Jehoshaphat's army faced overwhelming odds, they didn't send the warriors first—they sent the worshipers.

And when they lifted their voices, God sent an ambush from heaven.

They didn't draw a sword—just a song. And that song wrecked the enemy.

- Praise is a divine strategy.

- A supernatural sound.

- A heaven-born battle cry that causes confusion in the enemy's camp.

The Sound That Shakes Heaven and Earth

When you praise, it's not just emotion—it's motion.

- It moves angels.

- It stirs heaven.

- It shakes hell.

Walls don't fall because you admire them—they fall when you praise around them.

Jericho didn't fall because of military strength. It fell because of prophetic sound.

Praise Tells Hell You're Still Standing

Every time you praise, you send a message that says: *"I'm still here."*

- Despite the sickness.

- Despite the betrayal.

- Despite the lack.

- Despite the warfare.

Praise says: *"I'm not dead. I'm dangerous."*

When you forcefully and loudly proclaim the goodness of God, the world around you changes.

- You shift into attack mode.

- You go on the offensive.

- You move into battle against the minions of this world, and they run from you in fear.

You become a mighty warrior of the Lord God of all creation, and you march forward in His power and might.

- Angels respond.

- Demons tremble.

- Bondage breaks.

The devil doesn't fear your volume ...

... he fears your victory, wrapped in sound and blasted to the world, changing lives and circumstances.

Worship in Warfare

- When Paul and Silas praised, prison doors opened.

- When Joshua shouted, walls fell.

- When Jehoshaphat praised, enemies turned on themselves.

This isn't emotional hype. It's kingdom protocol.

Don't underestimate the power of your praise.

When you praise through pain, you prophesy to your future.

Praise As Prophecy Over Your Own Life

Your shout is not a show ...

... it's a strike.

Your worship isn't filler ...

... it's fire.

Your song is not secondary...

... it's supernatural.

So, sing like the walls around you depend on it.

Shout like the chains that have bound you are listening.

Praise like heaven is waiting to come to your aid.

Because it is.

Final Declaration

When you raise your voice in a shout of praise to the almighty God, hell backs up.

- Angels rise.

- Breakthrough comes.

- And once again, the rocks go silent.

The cause of hell's devastation is because you praised like a warrior ... and ...

ONE LESS STONE HAS TO SPEAK OUT IN PRAISE TO GOD.

Power Proclamation

"When I can't see the promise, I praise like I already possess it."

Pray With Me

Jesus, I choose to participate in the warfare and not just the warm-up.

Let my song of praise become a heavenly ambush to the evil one!

Turn the sound of my voice into a supernatural weapon for You.

Let the warfare of my praise elevate Your name before all the world.

Let me sing like my salvation depends on it, and let the walls obstructing Your will in my life come tumbling down! Amen.

Worship in Action

1. Join a prayer group. If your church doesn't have one, set one up. Open each session with a song of victory.

2. Plan a Jericho march in the Sunday night service. Invite the congregation to join in.

3. Join fellow believers for breakfast at a local restaurant. Open with prayer that everyone in the restaurant can hear.

— 9 —

Take Your Place—The Stone Can Wait

Don't Give Up Your Spot

Let everything that has breath praise the Lord. Praise the Lord!

— Psalm 150:6 —

- The invitation is open.

- The call is loud.

- The moment is now.

God is not looking for perfect voices.

He's looking for willing ones.

He's not waiting for the qualified.

He qualifies those who show up with a sound.

So, if you've been ...

- silent ...

- distracted ...

- discouraged ...

It's time to return to the altar with your voice.

You don't need to be flawless. You just need to be found praising.

You Were Born for This

Before you were ...

- a preacher ...

- a parent ...

- a leader ...

- a friend ...

. . . you were a worshiper.

Before you were known by *a title*, you were known by your sound.

God formed you in the womb, breathed His breath into your lungs, and handed you one primary assignment:

Praise.

- Your voice was wired to glorify God.
- Your lungs were built to release heaven.
- Your hands were made to lift high the King.

Don't waste the breath you were given on silence.

Stones Are Still Watching

Let's not forget, creation is still watching.

- The rocks haven't moved.
- The earth is still listening.
- The trees still tremble when glory comes near.

But the stones haven't cried out yet . . .

. . . because someone like you keeps showing up with a shout.

As long as the church is breathing, the rocks can keep waiting.

The Church Must Get Her Sound Back

It's not just about your personal praise …

… it's about a corporate cry.

The church must reverberate with praise.

Not just polished services, but presence-filled worship.

Not just programmed excellence, but prophetic expression.

- God is restoring the roar of the saints.

- He's reviving the sound of victory.

- He's raising up a generation that won't let rocks steal their role.

It can truly be said that the next revival won't be quiet.

It will ring with thunder that changes a generation.

Personal Activation and Encouragement

This is your time. This is your place. This is your

praise.

God wants you to:

- Step up.

- Step in.

- Speak out.

The altar is open. The King is listening. The rocks are waiting.

Today, the stone stays silent, because you found your shout and raised your praise to the almighty God.

That's one less stone …

BECAUSE YOU TOOK YOUR PLACE AT THE ALTAR OF PRAISE!

Power Proclamation

"As long as my heart is beating, that stone can sit right there."

Pray With Me

Jesus, I accept Your invitation to praise.

I want my voice to be loud. I desire to return to the altar with my voice.

I want to become known for my praise unto You.

Let the air in my lungs release the beauty of praise to everyone around me so that the stones at my feet remain silent.

Restore the roar of the saints and begin through me. Amen.

Worship in Action

1. Ask your pastor for a job no one else wants to do. Perform it as if Jesus is watching, because He is.

2. Visit an elderly care facility. Ask permission to have a praise opportunity for residents. Record their stories to post around the facility.

3. Volunteer to collect praise reports from the church body to include in the Sunday bulletin. E-mail them to members who can't make it to the service.

— 10 —

One Less Stone— Forever

Leave Your Stone Behind

And I heard, as it were, the voice of a great multitude, as the sound of many waters and as the sound of mighty thunderings, saying, "Alleluia! For the Lord God Omnipotent reigns!"

— Revelation 19:6 —

There's coming a day when the shout won't stop.

When the worship won't end.

When the sound of the redeemed will thunder like oceans and echo through eternity.

In that moment, when heaven's chorus erupts and crowns are cast before the throne, not one rock will be needed.

Every child of God, every blood-washed believer, and every Spirit-filled son and daughter will be lifting one voice, one sound, and one eternal song:

"Worthy is the Lamb!"

Heaven Isn't Quiet

When we reach heaven, we'll find it is:

- Full of worship.

- Full of voices.

- Full of praise.

There are things we'll never see, however. No matter where we look, we'll discover:

- No mute angels.

- No silent elders.

- No worship-less zones.

From Genesis to Revelation, every glimpse of God's presence involves sound:

- trumpets

- thunder

- roaring

- singing

- shouting

If you don't like praise, you won't enjoy heaven.

The truth found in God's Word tells us that eternity will be full of the sounds the enemy tried to silence while on this world.

Your Worship Leaves a Legacy

What you release now doesn't just echo in this life ... it rolls into the next. Your praise today is practice for the praise that never ends.

- When you choose worship instead of worry ...

- When you choose praise over pouting ...

- When you lift up Jesus despite your pain ...

You're writing a legacy that outlives you.

One day, I want my grandchildren to say, "We didn't inherit lots of money, but we inherited the sound of praise and worship to the King."

Make the Stone a Monument, Not a Substitute

There's nothing wrong with the stone as long as it stays silent.

Let your rock be a reminder, not a replacement.

Let it be a symbol of what could have been needed but wasn't.

Every time you see a stone, declare: "This one stayed quiet ... because I didn't."

Let each stone proclaim to the world: "This stone marks the spot where a person's praise silenced me."

A Lifestyle of Passionate, Daily Praise

This is not just a sermon.

Not just a book.

This is your eternal reminder that you were born

to praise.

- Let the angels sing.

- Let the elders bow.

- Let the saints roar.

And let every stone stand still.

Stand tall as you proclaim:

- "I have found my place."

- "I have found my voice."

- "I have found my fire."

And for the rest of your days … for all of eternity … that's one less stone that needs to cry out to God.

MAKE A COVENANT TO NEVER LET A ROCK CRY OUT IN YOUR PLACE.

Power Proclamation

"Let it be written in heaven's record: The stone stayed silent, because I didn't."

Pray With Me

Jesus, let the thunder of Your praise ring in my head.

Let me lift my voice with the believers to declare: "Worthy in the Lamb!"

Let me live in a zone of worship that is always filled with praise unto You.

Let me be aware of the legacy of worship that follows in my wake.

Let me declare that for all eternity, THIS STONE WILL BE SILENT. Amen.

Worship in Action

With your pastor's (and the city's) approval:

1. Initiate a project to rent a billboard to praise God for His goodness.

2. Take out an ad in the local paper to tell of the exploits of God among your congregation.

3. Print placards to display in church members' yards to lift the name of our holy God.

A Final Word

You can find Tim on the South Texas District website at www.stxag.org, on Facebook, or at his Houston office when he's not traveling his home state ministering in the churches across the South Texas District.

He'd be thrilled to connect with you and share stories of God's faithfulness.

Additional Books by
Tim R. Barker

If you liked this book, you may be interested in additional books Tim has written. Turn the page for a short description of each book. All are available on Amazon.

My *Jesus* Journey

This soul-building, introspective 4-book series reveals Tim's innermost heart on subjects that affect all of us, from Cooperation to Loyalty to The Truth of Salvation and more.

The books in this series include:

My Jesus Journey

My Jesus Journey: Crescendo

My Jesus Journey: Glissando

My Jesus Journey: Rhapsody

At *Your* Feet

In this book, you will read of God's favor and His redemption, for you are chosen and forgiven. In Jesus, you can find the rest you desire, for at His feet, His joy becomes whole.

Come to Jesus today. He holds His hand out to you.

From the Book of Hebrews
The Lord with Us

Do you have a relationship with Jesus? The rewards are great, but if we fail to heed the warnings in the Word, the consequences are also great.

Even if we call ourselves Christian, we must live according to God's will. The Lord is with us when we walk with Him. This is the message from the book of Hebrews.

Our Privilege of Joy

A Study of the Book of Philippians

Philippians is our blueprint from the Father, our plan for joy. It was written by the hand of Paul during his time in a Roman prison, but the voice is the Father's, entreating us to lift our hands in praise to Him, and to find joy even in the difficult parts of our lives.

NAMES OF GOD

Our name tells people who we are.

What about the name Christian? That's what the followers of Jesus call themselves. What information can people glean about us when we put a fish symbol on the bumper of our car, or we wear a cross around our neck? And, importantly, do our actions live up to their expectations?

This book is an in-depth teaching about the ten names of God.

THE VISION OF
NEHEMIAH
GOD'S PLAN FOR RIGHTEOUS LIVING

The Book of Nehemiah reveals a vital truth that our instant society often overlooks. Determination can take us only so far in achieving the goals God has for today's Church.

Winning the lost for Christ takes preparation in both our time and our finances. We become the "right stuff" for achieving God's plan when we are willing to risk everything for Him.

GOD'S REVELATION AND YOUR FUTURE

The book of Revelation is first and foremost a revelation about Jesus, not just the future.

John reveals Christ as the King of Glory, the conqueror, the one in charge of history, the one who alone controls the future, controls the nations, controls all the universe! This is the Jesus who is coming!

The book of Revelation shows us the glorified Christ and the certainty of His ruling over all things. We are not stumbling toward an uncertain future, but we must be in fellowship with the King!

Truth, Love & Redemption

The Holy Spirit For Today

There is no greater empowerment for the Christian of today than to seek out the Holy Spirit. It was considered vital in the early days of Christendom. Now, many times it is pushed aside as "for then" and not "for now."

We are in greater need of the truth, love, and redemption that flows from an encounter with the Holy Spirit than ever before. The Scriptures tell us that our realization of our need for Christ flows from the Spirit. Even before we accept Christ, the Holy Spirit draws us to Him.

The Call of Ephesians

Building the Church of Today

Paul understood that legalism can become a hindrance to our Christian walk and that we must focus on Christ and Christ alone. When our faith hits the road, God is there with us. He challenges us to trust Him to walk at our side through every challenge we might face.

When we do, we become mighty warriors in God's army.

That's Paul's message in a nutshell, and it's vital we take it to heart.

The Twelve
Taking up the Mantle of Christ

Twelve men were chosen to fulfill Christ's legacy on the earth.

Eleven looked to Jesus for the answers to life's questions. One chose the world and the world failed him.

These men were as varied as the members of our modern church, at times at odds with one another, but forged by Jesus into a single unit that overcame everything the devil could throw at them. What lesson can we learn from them?

Our only option is to choose Christ.

END TIMES

Scripture provides us a timeline of events that signal that the end is coming soon.

1. The Church Age
2. The Rapture of the Church
3. The Tribulation
4. The Second Coming of Jesus Christ
5. The Millennium
6. The Great White Throne Judgment
7. New Heavens and New Earth

Follow along through each of these Biblical timeline events.

Anticipating the Return of Christ

Are we waiting or are we watching for His appearance in the skies? The difference is in being ready for His return and risking missing Him altogether.

This book covers six areas of preparation for the Return of Christ.

1. Waiting
2. Mindful
3. Joyful
4. Praying
5. Thanking
6. Faithful.

Are you anticipating Christ's return? I am.

I *Your* Invitation ^{to} *Christ*

Your Invitation to Christ guarantees six things. Once you accept Christ's invitation you can:

1. Rest. It's yours in the midst of whatever comes your way.

2. See. Your eyes are opened to the supernatural.

3. Follow. Christ is your only true leader.

4. Drink. The ambrosia of Jesus becomes yours.

5. Dine. You will find renewal in your fellowship with your Lord.

6. Inherit. The Kingdom will one day be yours. It's called Heaven.

Salvation comes through Christ. God desires our presence, and we draw closer to Him through our Lord and Savior, Jesus.

The Authentic Christian

Revealing Christ through the Fruit of the Spirit

How do we prove who we say we are?

What's the secret to how it's done?

Is it in appearance? Actions that portray honesty?

How do we live out our Christian example, prove that we are who we say we are? What's our authentication, our password, our photo ID?

That's what this book is about, how we can live a real and honest Christian life that reflects the truth of Jesus living through us.

When you finish this book, you will understand what it means to be an authentic Christian.

UNIFIED CHURCH

The world cries out for your leadership as a Christ-driven example of how to find security and safety in Him.

We must band together arm-in-arm, hand-in-hand, our thoughts, compassion, and commitment to each other linked for a common goal we all share: spreading the message of salvation to a world that desperately needs to see the example of Jesus lived out through committed believers.

This book will become a useful tool to focus your witness to those around you and strengthen your relationship to your family, your involvement in your local body of believers and your commitment to Christ.

Mighty Men of Courage
From the Bible

Joseph who was sold into slavery. Daniel faced the lion's den. Abraham saw few of the promises of God during his lifetime. Moses lived for four decades in disgrace, an apparent failure.

Elijah hid in the desert with the ravens for three years, and Paul was arrested for his faith and thrown in prison. Repeatedly.

Yet today we recognize these men as courageous examples of faith in God. The difference is that they took a stand for God, looked beyond their personal circumstances and in faith allowed the hand of God to lead them.

Christ is calling. I want to answer.

Join me today, won't you?

Open Doors

Inside or outside. That's what a door conveys.

We can choose to stand on one side or the other. We can keep things inside or outside, open the door or close it. Some doors are found in opportunities, worship, or faithfulness. Then there are emotional doors. We can be locked in or out. The doors become prison bars, trapping us in painful situations.

Death is the final door in this life. Do you dread it or look forward to what's on the other side?

This book is your opportunity to discover how the doors in your life align with the Word of God. The choice is yours: inside or outside?

Decide for Jesus today. He is the only choice worth making. Christ is calling.

I want to answer. Join me today, won't you?

Reflecting Christ

—— through the ——

Fruit
of the
Spirit

The reflection we cast. Does it reveal us or Christ?

There is a distinction between outward appearances and true substance, and it's clear in how we live out our lives as followers of Jesus.

Why would the world accept a Christian who doesn't live like Christ? That's where the Fruit of the Spirit comes into play in our lives.

How do we know the Fruit is active in our lives? We see it in the love we show to those in need.

Decide for Jesus today. He is the only choice worth making.

CALLED CAMP
— 2025 —

Moses ... freeing the Egyptian slaves and parting the Red Sea!

David ... the King and the Psalmist!

Then there's Gideon, Jonah and Jeremiah!

Each of these men had to start somewhere small: Moses ran away to live in the desert. David tended sheep. Gideon, Jonah and Jeremiah just hoped to be left alone!

What has God called you to do for the kingdom? Are you willing to say yes?

Decide for Jesus today. He is the only choice worth making.

Discovering GOD in the Secret Places

The Word reveals to us that we will never have all the answers. God has set boundaries on our knowledge.

What seems right and appropriate for us, our families, and those we affect is based on feelings, circumstances, and the emotions that drive us to react rather than to reason.

We cry, "Where are you, God?" He whispers to us, "Slow down, and you will find me."

As you read this book, challenge yourself. Choose Wonder over Worry, bask in God's Season, and let the calendar of your life be written by the One who delivers us from a life of sin and shame.

Choose to trust in God, for He is the only one deserving of our eternal adoration.

It's Not All About Sitting at the Head Table

Here's what the example of Jesus teaches us: branding isn't enough. Wearing the Christian nametag is worthless if we don't hold up in the wash.

Do we feed the hungry? Do we clothe the naked? Are we a friend to the friendless and a comfort to the brokenhearted?

Jesus washed His disciples' feet. The Master stooped to the level of a servant, and in doing so, became a greater example of service than any soloist or evangelist ever dreamed.

The cost of leadership is heavy. The price for being "on show" rests hard on our shoulders.

Here's the lesson from our Lord:

To truly stand out in the Kingdom of God, we must first spend time on our knees.

www.ingramcontent.com/pod-product-compliance
Lightning Source LLC
Chambersburg PA
CBHW052009090426
42741CB00008B/1614